Table of Contents

Prologue

1. **Definition of Terms**

2. **Stopper Knots**
2.1 Overhand Knot
2.2 Double-Overhand Knot
2.3 Figure-Eight Knot
2.4 Slipknot

3. **Nooses**
3.1 Simple Noose
3.2 Slipped Noose
3.3 Double Fisherman's Loop
3.4 Running Bowline

4. **Loop Knots**
4.1 Overhand Loop
4.2 Figure-Eight Loop
4.3 Butterfly Knot
4.4 Moth Knot
4.5 Bowline
4.6 Bowline with the Yosemite-Tie Off
4.7 Double-Bowline
4.8 Triple-Bowline
4.9 In Line Figure-Eight
4.10 Double Figure-Eight Loop
4.11 Blake Loop

5. **Hitches**
5.1 Clove Hitch
5.2 Hamburger Clove Hitch
5.3 Timber Hitch
5.4 Constrictor Knot
5.5 Lingens Knot
5.6 Girth Hitch
5.7 Cow Hitch
5.8 Buntline Hitch
5.9 Anchor Hitch
5.10 Munter Hitch

6. **Bends**
6.1 Overhand Bend
6.2 Water Knot and Flemish Bend
6.3 Sheet Bend and Double-Sheet Bend
6.4 Quick Hitch
6.5 Double-Fisherman's Knot
6.6 Double-Buntline
6.7 Beer Knot

7. **Climber's Friction Hitches**
7.1 Prusik
7.2 Swabian Prusik
7.3 Klemheist
7.4 Blake
7.5 Bachmann Hitch and Hansa Hitch
7.6 Machard
7.7 Distel
7.8 Saxon Prusik
7.9 Happy
7.10 Very Happy
7.11 Howard Hitch
7.12 Valdotain Braid
7.13 Knut

8. **Various**
8.1 Met one, met 'em all
8.2 Bread and Butter
8.3 Gasket Hitch

9. **Safety Knots**
9.1 Stopper Knots
9.2 Half-Hitch and Slipped Half-Hitch
9.3 Half-Knot and Single Bow
9.4 Barrel Knot

10. Sources

11. Thanks

Prolog

Perhaps climbing arborists and their grounds people are some of the last professions that still rely daily on a wide assortment of knots. It is easier to tackle various problems, if the repertoire of solutions is large. "Knots" is a wide-ranging subject, and the examples in this book are just the tip of the iceberg. For every possible knot dilemma there is more than one knot that can solve it, and most knots have more than one use. My goal is to highlight the most used and the most practical examples for the tree-climbing profession. It is not a requirement that every one of these examples becomes part of your accumulated skills but hopefully you can find the right ones to simplify your workday.

Included here are a few "new" knots, that I hope you can find a use for. I, personally would be delighted to learn of knots used in the profession that are not found in this manual. They could possibly find a place in the next edition.

The specific properties of the knots in this manual are dependent on the use of a semi-static synthetic kernmantle cord. When using other rope types it is important to be aware that the properties of the knots may change.

Before using a knot, it is important to be sure that your application corresponds to the function.

As far as knot names go, I stuck pretty close to Ashley (ref. 10. Sources), unless another name is more common in the tree climbing profession. I have made an effort to avoid false or confusing information. With other possible names that are not frequently used in the climbing scene and could be considered irrelevant, I have taken the freedom and left them out. The theme "knots" is not a science and thus is not systematic like Botany or Zoology.

The explanations of the knots are organized under the headings: **Other Names, Explanation, Use, The Pluses, The Minuses, Worth Noting.** When irrelevant, headings are left out.

About Other Names:
As already mentioned, This subject remains sparse. Under this heading some knots are categorized as "first appearance". This does not necessarily mean that the knot is brand new. Such an assumption could not be proven.

About Explanation:
There are often many methods to tie the same knot. Because it would be overtly extensive and counter productive to count off every single method, I have decided to give at least one easy to follow example. After all, it's the results that counts.

About Use:
Some of the uses in this book may be alien to some readers. It is possible that this "use" is a solution to a problem that has not yet appeared. Hopefully, if the problem arises, the use will clarify itself and the solution will become clear.

About The Pluses / The Minuses:
One mans heaven is another mans hell. So don't sue me if you disagree with my prognosis.

About Worth Noting:
Like the title suggests, this is the spot for interesting and notable facts that may simplify your work day, or just make reading more enjoyable.

So pick up some rope (preferably a 2 meter long 8 mm thick accessory cord) and practice.

1 Definition of Terms

There are three steps to binding a knot: tie, dress and set. The end result is either correct or incorrect. There is no "almost" correct. As a general safety rule the loose end of the rope should stick out of the knot at least 10-times the rope diameter.

1.1 Standing end and loose end:
The standing end of the rope is the part of the rope that is already or will come under tension after tying the knot. The loose end is the part of the rope that is not under tension. It is the part that would be used to tie the knot and is usually the shorter part of the rope. That is not always the case! For example with the Simple Noose (3.1) where the standing end is slipped. When climbing with the Doubled-Rope Climbing Technique, the loose end of the rope can be very long.

Traditionally there are more terms connoting other parts of the rope, but for the here mentioned knots these two terms are sufficient for clear instruction. Furthermore the basic logic of the terms make them easy to remember.

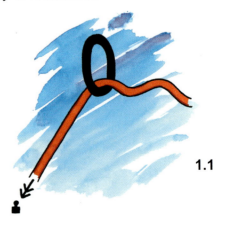

1.1

1.2 Bight: a double section of rope, often mid line, that does not cross itself

1.2

1.3 Loop: when a bight is twisted, causing the rope to cross over itself

1.3

1.4 Turn: a loop around another object, it is called a turn

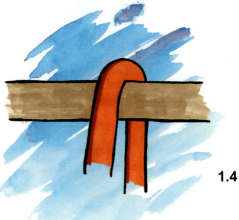

1.4

1.5 Round Turn: The rope is turned 1.5 times around an object. A round turn can be applied as a Hitch (5.).

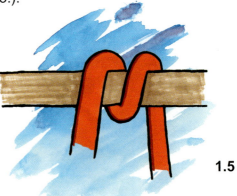

1.5

1.6 Eye: (not illustrated) Any time that the rope curves in on itself, joining or crossing, it forms a hole, or an eye. This term applies to a loop, a noose, a loop knot, or a splice.

1.7 Rope Ends: Shown are three various rope ends:
a. when the knot can only be tied with a rope end
b. when the knot may be tied midline
c. when the knot is typically but not necessarily tied with the rope end

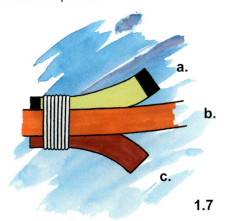

1.7

1.8 Slip or slipping a knot: A slip is, in effect, a draw loop. For example when tying an Overhand Knot (2.1), instead of finishing the knot by tucking the end, one forms a bight in the end and tucks this instead (2.4 or 3.1). By pulling the slipped end the knot unravels.

1.9 Laid or tucked: (not illustrated) To lay a knot means to tie it on a bight. To tuck a knot means to tie it around an object.

2 Stopper Knots

Stopper knots are made in ropes, usually at the end, with the result that the bulkiness of the knot stops the rope from slipping through the pulley, ring, or your friction hitch. A Loop Knot (4.) could also function as a stopper.

2.1 Overhand Knot

Other names: Single-Overhand Knot, Thumb Knot

Use: This is the easiest and smallest of the stopper knots. It is helpful for pulling one's friction saver out of the tree. One must be careful using this knot as a stopper knot at the end of ones climbing line. Unlike the Double-Overhand Knot (2.2), the Overhand Knot is not secure, i.e. it easily loosens itself, and thus requires periodical controlling. Another security measure would be to allow a meter long loose end behind the knot.

Pluses: It is easy and fast.

Minuses: It easily spills.

Worth Noting:
The Overhand Knot is the starting point for many knots.

2.1

2.2 Double-Overhand Knot

Other names: Blood Knot, Multiple Overhand Knot

Explanation: formed either like figure 2.2.1 or 2.2.2; with figure 2.2.2 make sure that the eye is large enough to allow for the knot to flip into place. Figure 2.2.3 is an example of a well-ordered Double-Overhand Knot (with a bulge left and a bulge right of the bridging rope), whereas figure 2.2.4 is not well ordered (with two bulges on one side of the bridge).

Use: securest stopper knot for the end of your climbing rope

Pluses: long lasting

Minuses: The knot is relatively bulky. After being pulled tight, it can be hard to open.

2.2.1

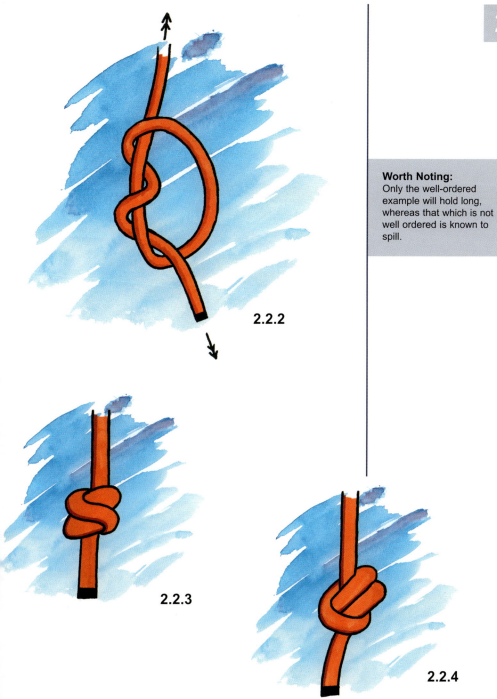

Worth Noting:
Only the well-ordered example will hold long, whereas that which is not well ordered is known to spill.

2.2.2

2.2.3

2.2.4

2.3 Figure-Eight Knot

Use: This can be used as a stopper in your climbing rope. The security of this knot lies between the Overhand Knot (2.1) and the Double-Overhand (2.2) Knot.

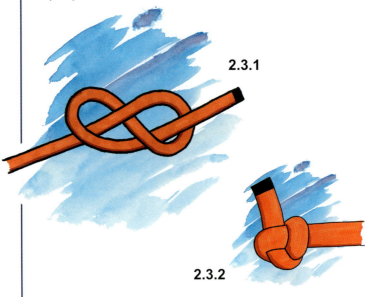

2.3.1

2.3.2

2.4 Slipknot

Other name: Slipped Overhand Knot

Explanation: Tie an Overhand Knot (2.1), and slip the loose end (2.4.1 and 2.4.2). When the standing end is pulled the knot remains intact, as opposed to the Simple Noose (3.1).

Use: It is used as a temporary handle in the throw line (the knot should lie at a length of 50-100cm from the throw bag, and acts as a handle). When

Worth Noting:
If it is possible, do not pull the knot too tight, so it can be easily released.

the rigging rope is being pulled up to the block, the ground man ties a Slipknot to stop the rope from falling through. The loose end needs to be long enough that the climber can reach it, plus 1-2 meters for fastening a hitch to the branch (5.7.3).

Pluses: fast to tie

Minuses: This knot is easily confused with the Simple Noose: For example when a chainsaw is hung in a Slipknot, there is a good chance that it will fall down (broken chainsaw, broken helmet, broken head).

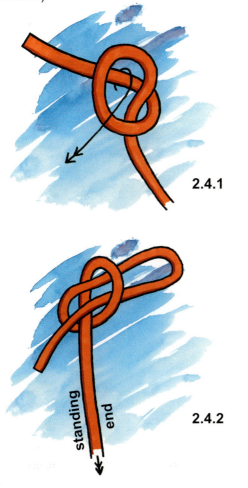

2.4.1

2.4.2

3 Nooses

The eye of a noose closes when the standing end of the rope is pulled.

3.1 Simple Noose

Other name: Noose

Explanation: Tie an Overhand Knot (2.1), and slip the standing end (3.1.1 and 3.1.2). When the standing end of the rope is pulled the eye tightens and the knot spills, as opposed to the Slipknot (2.4). This knot can be easily laid as well as tucked.

Use: hooking up tools and ropes onto a rope to be hoisted up to the climber

Pluses: quick to tie

Minuses: This knot is easily mistaken with the Slipknot (2.4): If the rigging rope is pulled up to the block with a Simple Noose, chances are that the noose unravels and the rope falls through. With stiff or thick rope, the Simple Noose can push open a snap carabiner.
Here it is safer to use the Double-Fisherman's Loop (3.3).

3.1.1

3.1.2

3.2 Slipped Noose

Other name: Halter Hitch

Use: This is "The Knot" for attaching your throw bag to your throw line. (The Cow Hitch (5.7) ties quicker but is not as quick to untie and doesn't hold on all throw lines.)

Pluses: secure and easy to open

Minuses: The critics are still searching.

Worth Noting:
This can be confused with a Slipped Half-Hitch (9.2), which may not hold on a throw line.

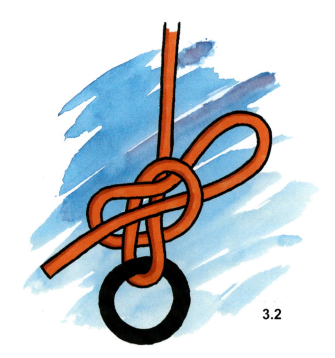

3.2

3.3 Double-Fisherman's Loop

Other Name: Poacher's Knot

Explanation: a Double-Overhand Knot (2.2) tied with a slipped standing end

Use: end of line attachment; it lets itself tie well with thick or stiff ropes when hoisting tools into the tree; as a rope termination for the accessory cord ends on your climber's friction hitch (ref. Very Happy 7.10)

Pluses: a very tight noose that cinches up on the carabiner

Minuses: tight enough that it could be hard to open; if one tries to tie this but slips the loose end instead of the standing end, the knot will open under load like a Slipknot (2.4).

Worth Noting:
As with the Double-Overhand Knot check that the knot is well ordered, to ensure a good hold.

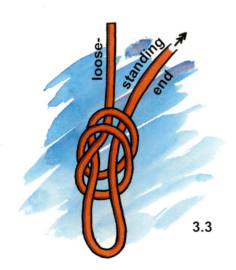

3.3

3.4 Running Bowline (ref. Bowline (4.5))

Worth Noting: When rigging branches it could be tied in place of a Timber Hitch with a Half-Hitch in the standing end (5.3). This reduces the possibility of the branch ripping down to the main knot and thus minimizes an accident.

Explanation: Tie a Bowline with its eye around its standing end.

Use: an important knot to attach branches; it makes it possible to rig branches from a distance. Throw the rope over the designated branch (probably using the Bread and Butter (8.2)), take the loose end, tie your bowline around the standing end and pull tight. It also works well for anchoring an access line to the tree trunk for a single rope ascent (be sure to secure; ref. fig. 4.5.3 or 4.6.2).

Pluses: As explained in "Use" it can be installed from a distance. Remains easy to open even after heavy loads.

Minuses: Please refer to the Bowline.

3.4

Loop Knots 4

Loop knots form one or more secure eyes. Regardless of the load or the objekt to which it is tied the eye remains the same size – as opposed to nooses (3.) or hitches (5.).

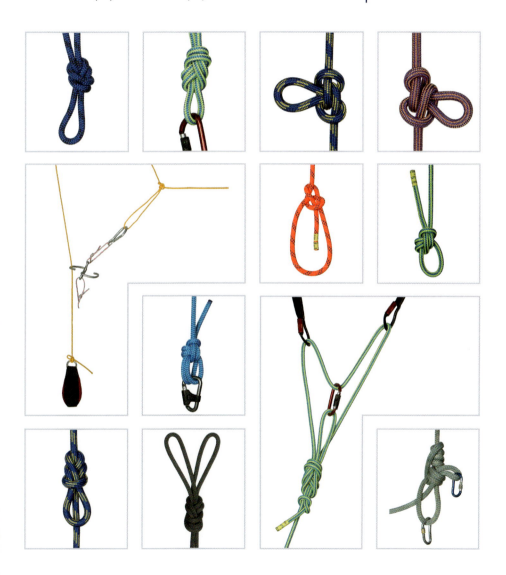

4.1 Overhand Loop

Other names: Loop Knot, Overhand on a Bight

Explanation: This is an Overhand Knot (2.1) tied with a bight.

Use: only to be used in an emergency as an end of line attachment; easy to form an eye mid-rope for pulling tools up

Pluses: easy, quick and secure

Minuses: When it has been under tension it is hard to open.

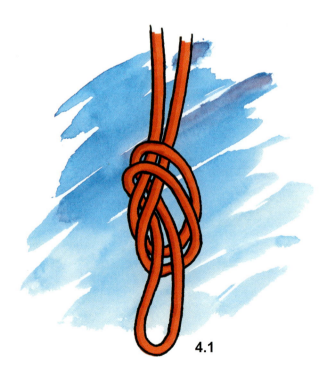

4.1

4.2 Figure-Eight Loop

Other names: Flemish Loop, Figure-Eight on a Bight

Explanation: It is a Figure-Eight (2.3) tied with the bight (4.2.1 and 4.2.2).

Use: end of line attachment knot

Pluses: easier to open than an Overhand Loop (4.1)

Minuses: A well-ordered Figure-Eight Loop requires practice.

Worth Noting: very popular end of line attachment knot amongst beginners; with an extra turn of the loop you have a Figure-Nine Loop (4.2.3). Yet another turn will give you the Figure-Ten Loop (not illustrated). Trying to tuck the Figure-Ten Loop is something for the kid with first prize in the geometry contest.

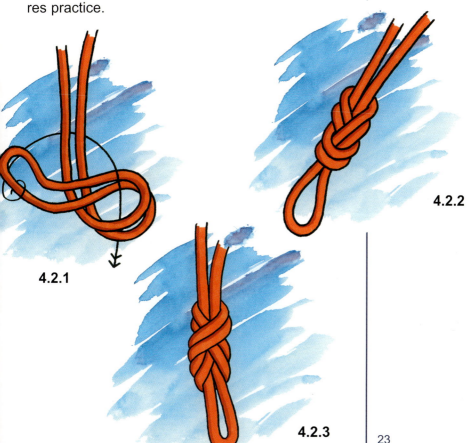

4.2.1

4.2.2

4.2.3

4.3 Butterfly Knot

Worth Noting:
Don't confuse this with the Moth Knot (4.4), even when they are often sold in one package.

Other Names: Harness Loop, Lineman's Loop, Artillery Man's Hitch

Explanation: This can be tied either like diagrams 4.3.1.1 → 4.3.2 → 4.3.3 or like diagrams 4.3.1.2 → 4.3.2 → 4.3.3, but never like 4.4.1. Notice the small differences in the results.

Use: a mid-line knot; either pulled into the tree to choke the rope used for the ascent or for hanging a pulley for a mechanical advantage system (although the In Line Figure-Eight Loop (4.9) is prettier)

Pluses: Both ends exit the knot in the direction of the pull.

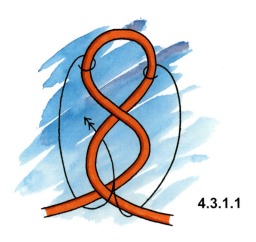

4.3.1.1

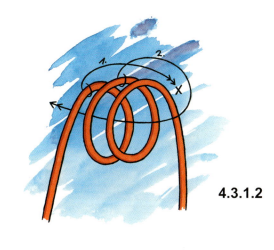

4.3.1.2

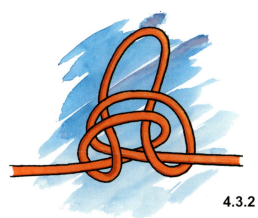

4.3.2

4.3.3

4.4 Moth Knot

Other Names: This is tied like the Englishman's Knot (not illustrated) but dressed differently. I have given it the new name, but it might also be a Capsized Englishman's Knot. Once again, this is not the Butterfly Knot (4.3).

Explanation: Can be tied either like figure 4.4.1 or like figure 4.4.2, which is a Slipknot (2.4) with an extra Half-Hitch (9.2) around the eye. When tying the second way take notice of the direction of the Half-Hitch.

Use: If you are in a tree, and you've thrown your throw line into the neighboring tree, this knot could be used to attach a small grappling hook for getting the throw line back to you.

Pluses: easy to untie; The size of the eye is easy to regulate when tying Slipknots mid-line (which is necessary when using a small grappling hook).

Minuses: a rarely useful knot

Worth Noting:
If you don't have a grappling hook then you don't need the Moth Knot, but never forget its contrasts to the Butterfly Knot, which is often handy.

4.4.1

4.4.2

4.5 Bowline

Other Names: Bowling, Bolin or Standing Bowline

Explanation: First form a loop in the rope. If the standing end lays at the bottom of the loop then run the loose end from underneath up through the eye of the loop (or vice versa). From here, run the loose end around the standing end and back through the loop so that it runs parallel to itself. Make sure that it runs on the inner side of the line first entering the loop. By pulling the loose and standing ends, the knot is set.

The common story with the snake (or alligator) does not necessarily help if he does not know where the tree is.

If the loose end is laid on the inside than it is a good Bowline, but if it is laid on the outer edge, it is a Left-hand Bowline (bad). (Ref. chapter 8.1)

Just a tip: Make the first loop relatively small and make the loop that forms the final binding eye big. It makes the tying easier and more organized.

A Bowline can also be tied by running the loose end through a Simple Noose (3.1) something like

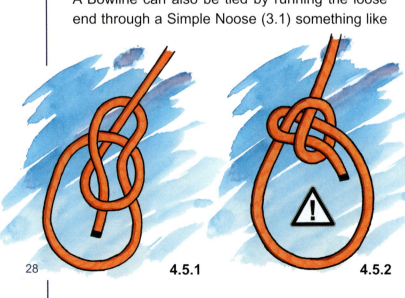

4.5.1   **4.5.2**

fig. 6.3.2, but be careful that the outcome is a Bowline.

Use: as an end of line attachment, especially when the rope needs to be tied around an object, due to the Bowline's ability to be stuck as well as tied; for extra security, either use the Yosemite-Tie Off (4.6) which works well if the knot is constantly in motion (as with a climbing system). Or use a Half-Knot (9.3) like fig 4.5.3, if the Bowline remains under tension without motion. In such a case a Left-hand Bowline with a Half-Knot would also suffice. If the knot is only temporarily in action (for example when rigging a branch), then it can be used without a back up knot. Anchor point for SRT industrial access work.

Pluses: Even after heavy loading, the knot remains easy to untie; easy and quick to tuck; loop size is easily adjusted

Minuses: If it isn't secured and isn't kept under tension, it has a tendency to creep, distort, and even unravel. It doesn't react well to cross loading of the eye (for example two anchor points in one eye).

Worth Noting:
There are many sorts of bowlines. Figure 4.5.2, the Eskimo Bowline, looks like the Simple Bowline but isn't. This knot is absolutely not to be recommended for securing people, but would be interesting to test, because the problems of cross loading the eye, doesn't seem to occur (a similar knot appears later under the variation of the Sheet Bend in figure 6.3.3.).
The Eskimo Bowline is good to set a static removable false crotch, although it is preferable to make a double loop at the start (4.5.4; ref. Double-Sheet Bend (6.3.4)).

4.5.3

4.5.4

29

4.6 Bowline with the Yosemite-Tie Off

Explanation: The loose end leaves the knot parallel to the standing end (4.6.1 and 4.6.2), easy, cheesy.

Use: if the Bowline (4.5) is in motion or not under a constant load

Pluses: the eye remains free; a compact knot

Minuses: requires a keen sense of distances; there are many ways to leave the knot.
Warning: In an effort to keep the knot small one runs the risk of hanging ones weight in the wrong loop (4.6.3).

Worth Noting:
For the discovery of the Dead Yosemite-Bowline (4.6.4) many thanks are owed Christine Engel (Tree Climbing Instructor). In a test situation, one of the candidates tied a proper Bowline with the Yosemite-Tie Off, as I could see from out of the tree. The candidate dressed the knot a little, and when Christine checked the knot, alas it failed the test. I later tried to reconstruct the knot and ended up with the Dead Yosemite-Bowline. Remove the security and it becomes clear what the mistake is. In the past few years there has been a number of accidents with this knot.

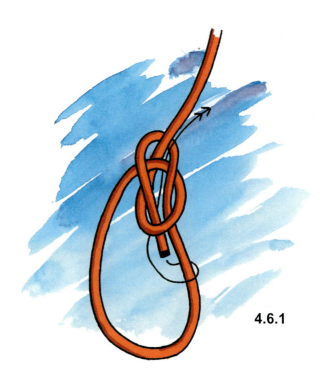

4.6.1

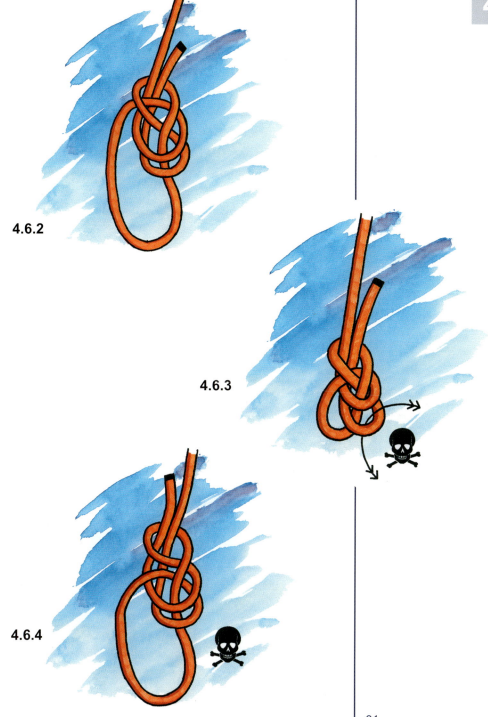

4.6.2

4.6.3

4.6.4

4.7 Double-Bowline

Explanation: Start to tie a Bowline (4.5) with a bight, but instead of running the "loose end" around the standing end and entering the single turn for the second time, wrap the eye of the loose end around the entire knot (final termination eye and loop), and pull the knot tight (4.7.1 and 4.7.2). This knot can also be formed by tucking the loose end of a bowline, in which case it is unimportant whether it's a Left-hand Bowline or a Bowline proper.

Use: end of line attachment; it can be helpful to have two loops handy when pulling.

Pluses: It can be tied mid-rope. It's easy to untie and doesn't need added security. The knot doesn't even distort if one accidentally loads only one of the loops.

Minuses: If tension is applied to the standing end before it is dressed and set, it can capsize forming a noose (3.). (Just for the record, even when this happens, the knot remains secure.)

Worth Noting:
If the Bowline with the Yosemite-Tie Off (4.6) or the security in figure 4.5.3, is giving you a headache, this knot is a substantial alternative. It is just as easy, fast to tie and remains secure, but it is a little bulkier.

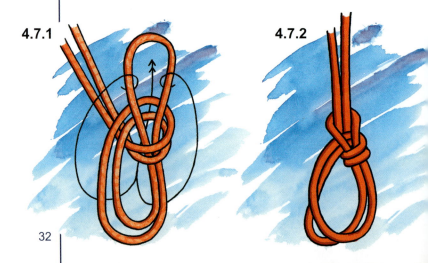

4.7.1

4.7.2

4.8 Triple-Bowline

Explanation: Simply tie a Bowline (4.5) with a bight of rope. The "loose end" is the third loop (4.8.1 and 4.8.2).

Use: when even more people are pulling on the line; it is also possible to use knots with four or more loops, but in such cases it is probably safer to work with a mechanical advantage system, giving you a more controlled pull and hindering rocking the tree. This minimizes the possibility of the tree falling in the wrong direction, just in case the weight, angle and wind were not properly judged. This knot could also substitute a climbing harness (2 legs, a waist and a loose end for a Climber's Friction Hitch), in case you find yourself without.

Pluses: many secure eye loops

Minuses: a big knot that uses a lot of rope

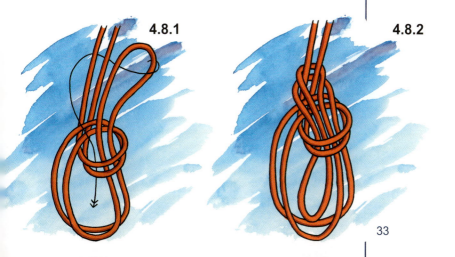

4.8.1   4.8.2

4.9 In Line Figure-Eight Loop

Other Names: Ashley leaves it nameless simply calling it the Bowline with a Bight, but it is worth more than that.

Explanation: See figures 4.9.1 and 4.9.2.

Use: a good loop for attaching a mechanical advantage system to a rope; due to the run of the rope and its ability to be easily tied and untied, it is superior to the Butterfly Knot (4.3). It is also good to choke an access rope against the branch for footlocking.

Pluses: nice run of the rope

Minuses: With minimal changes one can end up with a different knot. Should be loaded only in one direction.

Worth Noting:
But she's a looker, ain't she?

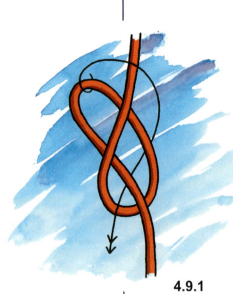

4.9.1

4.9.2

4.10 Double Figure-Eight Loop

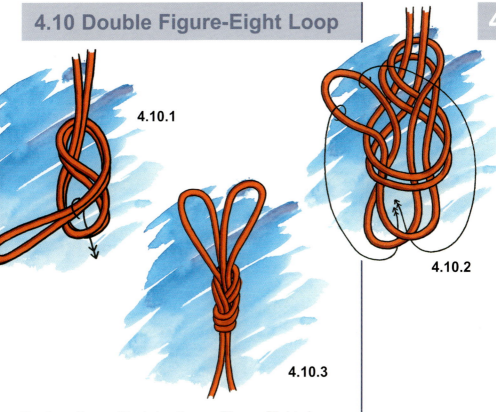

Explanation: Start to tie a Figure-Eight Loop (4.2), but slip the "loose end". The eye of this "loose end" should then be flipped around the entire knot (4.10.1 and 4.10.2). Figure 4.10.3 shows the final knot.

Use: good for pulling with two people; used by high access workers to achieve a load sharing anchor point

Pluses: The loops are mutually adjustable, make one bigger and the other becomes smaller.

Minuses: As opposed to the Double-Bowline, this knot might deform if only one loop is loaded: This knot can capsize and unravel.

Worth Noting:
In German it is known as Hasenohrenknoten (Rabbit Ear Knot ref. 4.10.3).

4.11 Blake Loop (ref. Blake (7.4))

Other Names: probably not the first appearance, but a new name

Explanation: Tie a Blake around its own standing end (4.11.1). It is better to wrap the rope a few times more than less, to avoid a Blake Noose. If tying mid-rope, then slip the loose end, as shown in figure 4.11.2. The slipped end can be secured with a carabiner, for example.

Use: For someone that needs an eye that can take the pressure.

Pluses: high breaking strain; easy to open even after loading; can be tied mid-rope

Minuses: more complicated than the other loops

Worth Noting:
When tested on a 8mm accessory cord, this knot offered a 50% higher breaking strain than a Bowline (4.5) or a Figure-Eight Loop (4.2).
The Blake Loop has already made it to the cover of a famous book of knots ☺

4.11.1

4.11.2

Hitches

5 Hitches

Hitches are knots tied on or around other objects. Without the object, hitches collapse.

5.1 Clove Hitch

Other name: Waterman's Knot

Explanation: tied around an object or tied on the bight and placed over the object (5.1.1 or 5.1.2)

Use: end of line attachment; if the rope is securing a person, then always add a backup knot for security, for example: with the Half-Knot, as in figure 5.1.4, or the Barrel Knot (9.4).
When used in a transitional climbing system and is tied directly to your harness d-ring, the Blake, tied in the loose end, works well as the friction hitch (7.4.2); works well for rigging, even with multiple branches

Pluses: quick; able to be tied one handed

Minuses: As easy as it is, it's just as easy to tie it wrong. If it is tied on a bight and put into a carabiner, there are just minor differences between the round turn (1.5), the Girth Hitch (5.6), the Munter Hitch (5.10), and the Clove Hitch.
The bigger the object to which one hitches, the easier it is for the knot to distort and unravel. Hence it is mandatory that this knot is backed up with a safety knot.

Worth Noting:
When rigging branches it is important to make sure that the branch does not tear which may capsize a Clove Hitch. A Half-Hitch (9.2) in the standing end, as with the Timber Hitch (5.3), will minimize this danger. If you're not rigging branches at the center of gravity (which is usually the case), then it is crucial that the directions of the loose end and standing end are taken into consideration (5.1.3). The same applies when attaching your rope to the throw line, before pulling it up into the tree.

5.1.1

5.1.2

5.1.3

5.1.4

5.2 Hamburger Clove Hitch

Explanation: Method # 1 (5.2.1): Tie a Clove Hitch (5.1), tie the loose ends together into an end to end hitch and adjust the knot so that it's on the opposite side of the stem to the Clove Hitch.

Method # 2 (5.2.2): Lay a turn around the object. On the one side of the turn form a loop as pictured. The turn continues into a round turn (1.5) with the rope passing through the loop. Both loose ends are then tied on the opposite side of the object from the loop. Then comes the question "which knot is the best end to end hitch". In figure 5.2.1 we have a Sheet Bend (6.3.1). Another possibility is to run one end through a loop knot, turn it back on itself and secure it with two Half-Hitches (9.2).

Not tested but perhaps interesting is the following knot: Tie a Slipknot (2.4) (not a Simple Noose as in figure 6.3.2), run the second end through and pull the loose end until it flips into place. What you have is a Lock Knot (6.3.3). (See also the Eskimo-Bowline (4.5.2).) The beauty of this is the opportunity to control the size of the eye while still having the rope tightly hug the object to which you have hitched.

Use: when a high breaking strain is required, for example when securing a mechanical advantage system or a rigging block

Pluses: a very high breaking strain so long the hitch is evenly stressed; this is due to the fact that the turns are not tight and that the finishing knot lies where it can least weaken the whole system.

Minuses: It at first comes across as a peculiar knot to tie, even in spite of the clear description under "explanation".

5.2.1

Worth Noting:
This knot was shown to me by Lutz Hoffman (in cooperation with his rope specialist, Jochen Gnass). It has a lot of potential. The idea of placing the knot where it doesn't get in the way (see also Prusik (7.1)), helps for efficient work.

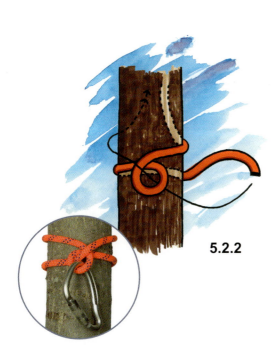

5.2.2

5.3 Timber Hitch

Explanation: The loose end has to be wrapped at least one-third of the circumference of the object and consist of at least three round turns. A stopper knot can be tied in the loose end. Because the knot is often only shortly in use, an Overhand Knot (2.1) would suffice.

Use: end of line attachment for rigging; not to be used for personal protection (see "minuses")

Pluses: Even after application of a heavy load, the knot easily opens.

Minuses: This knot is susceptible to direction changes in the standing end, which in the worst case scenario, could lead to a bunching of the round turns, consequently minimizing the hold on the object. To hinder this it is advisable to place a Half-Hitch (9.2) in the standing end as in fig. 5.3 (Timber Hitch with a Half-Hitch). (Ref. Running Bowline (3.4).) It is further not recommended that the rope is pulled forward (away from the page, referring to the figure), for example when pulling a tree over. The turns are no longer all held snug, and it could be that the knot spills.

Worth Noting:
When tying a redirect pulley in the outer branches of a tree, it is important to take into account that the direction of pull could change. In this case a Half-Hitch is no longer sufficient security. It is either necessary to add a few more turns or to use an alternative. (Ref. Cow Hitch (5.7).)

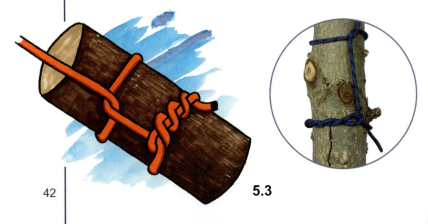

5.3

5.4 Constrictor Knot

Explanation: Either tie a Clove Hitch (5.1) and pass one loose end under one of the turns (5.4.1), or simply lay the Constrictor (5.4.2 - 5.4.4).

Use: for tying smooth objects, like your thermos; for tying the throw line to the rope; the start of the Lingens Knot (5.5)

Pluses: simple and elegant

Minuses: can pull itself too tight

Worth Noting: With a little practice, the knot is tied in three seconds.

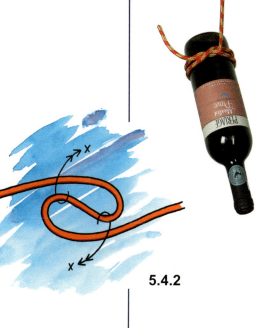

5.4.1 5.4.2

5.4.3 5.4.4

5.5 Lingens Knot

Other names: first appearance

Explanation: similar to the Constrictor (5.4); the knot is tied loosely in a carabiner. Pull first on the standing end until the knot flips over into place, then pull the knot tight on the loose and standing ends. This flip is important because the constrictor could later flip over if one sided tension is applied. At this point, the knot may loosen. The Lingens Knot must then be backed with a stopper knot. Another fine back up is a carabiner 50 mm key pierced through the loose end (5.5) 10 cm from the rope end. The carabiner, or Overhand Knot, works fine for later removing your friction saver from the tree.

Use: end of line attachment for softer ropes in carabiners

Worth Noting:
Start using this knot slowly and then feel the satisfaction. The results of the load tests can be seen at www.kletterdienste.de (with the friendly support of the company Edelmann and Ridder).

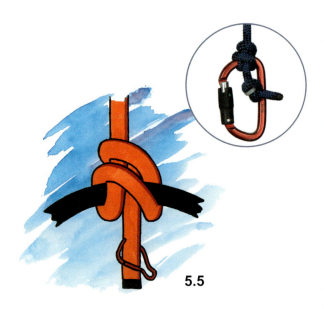

5.5

Pluses: fast to tie; hugs a carabiner tightly; if you are climbing with a split-tail-system, there is the elegant possibility to take the sling between the two turns of the Lingens Knot to fix yourself on the carabiner.

Minuses: This is only for softer ropes. Stiff ropes can't be tightened enough, when the rope loosens, the carabiner can rotate so that it snags on the gate.

5.6 Girth Hitch

Other name: Ring Hitch

Use: to tie up slings that need to choke the rope

Pluses: fast and it's impossible to do it wrong

Minuses: If your rope slips over your figure-eight when descending, it proves a very effective but annoying brake.

Worth Noting:
Normally the Girth Hitch, in contrast to the Cow Hitch (5.7), is usually tucked or laid with a bight, with both ends receiving load. However the two knots look identical.

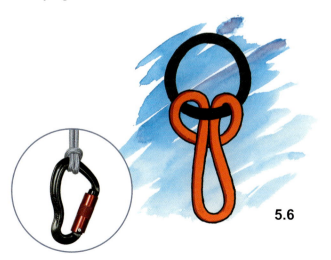

5.6

5.7 Cow Hitch

Explanation: customarily a Girth Hitch (5.6) tucked with one loose end; the loose end is commonly secured with a Half-Hitch (9.2) (5.7.1). In the diagram the Cow Hitch is tied starting underneath and coming out on top. Vice versa holds snugger (as with a Clove Hitch (ref. 5.1.3)), but because the knot is often used with heavier objects, for example a heavy-duty rigging block, the shown method is easier to tie in the tree. An extra Half-Hitch (5.7.2) heightens security. Whether it is on the right or left or only around one rope is unimportant. When attaching a Lowering Device (for example a Port-A-Wrap) figure 5.7.1 is optimal because the pull is coming from above, thus holding the knot snug against the trunk.

Use: to attach pulleys or lowering devices, etc; to attach a throw bag, but be careful because it may eventually be difficult to untie and does not hold on all lines; (Ref. Slipped Noose (3.2).)

Pluses: easier to pull tight and adjust than the Timber Hitch (5.3)

Minuses: The rope has to travel twice around the object and this requires a lot of rope. After heavy load, the Cow Hitch is harder to open than the Timber Hitch. In relation to the figures, when the pull comes from underneath, or from the diagram's left, then there are no worries for the security of the knot. However if the pull is from the right, there

Worth Noting:
The Cow Hitch is superior to the Timber Hitch in many aspects, but can never replace it.
In figure 5.7.3 a rigging block is secured with a dead eye sling made with an Overhand Loop (4.1). It is important that the eye remains big: First, it allows the Cow Hitch to choke under load without being blocked by the loop knot. Second, the impact load is distributed over two parts of the rope as well as being absorbed by friction on the object before entering the Overhand Loop, which has an low breaking strain. The same applies to a splice (5.10.3).

is the danger that the loop can slip out and that the knot could open up. This is important to note when attaching a redirect pulley in the outer branches of a tree. 5.7.2 is very secure but to use a Munter Hitch with two Half-Hitches (5.10.3) is even better in such a situation.

5.7.1

5.7.2

5.7.3

5.8 Buntline Hitch

Explanation: Tie a self locking Clove Hitch (5.1.3) with the loose end on the standing end of the rope.

Use: end of line attachment

Pluses: good to tightly fix a carabiner; always easy to loosen

Minuses: When tying this knot it is easy to make a mistake.

Worth Noting:
Normally it is not necessary to secure this knot.
If seen as necessary, than a Stopper Knot (9.1) will suffice.
The Buntline could also be seen as a noose (3.), but due to its characteristics and its uses, it is placed under the hitches.

5.8

5.9 Anchor Hitch

Explanation: tucked or laid; when the second is done, simply place the carabiner into a badly ordered Double-Overhand Knot (2.2.4).

Use: end of line attachment

Pluses: good for fixing a carabiner; easy to picture and carry out; always easy to open

Minuses: Because this knot is not as tight as others, it is important that it is secured, for example a Stopper Knot (9.1).

Worth Noting:
Instead of laying a carabiner in a badly ordered Double-Overhand Knot, try a well-ordered one (2.2.3). The result is a related knot that has a certain superficial similarity to the Lingens Knot (5.5). Both this knot and the Anchor Hitch, however, do not hug a carabiner as tightly as the Lingens Knot.

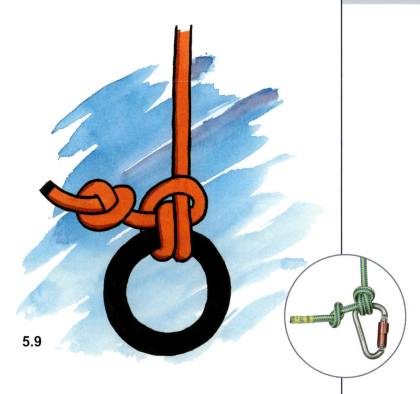

5.9

5.10 Munter Hitch

Worth Noting:
Such a useful knot that it's mandatory climber's knowledge.

Other name: Crossing Knot

Explanation: either laid around a carabiner or laid in the hand and placed on a carabiner; one can also tuck this knot.

Use: This knot has two very different possibilities. a) adds controlled friction to a system for a smoother fall and minimized shock loads to the rope (5.10.1); light rigging; belaying people, but always backed up by a suitable self belay; an additional turn on the load end increases the friction (5.10.2). Normally either the Single-Bow (9.3.2) or the Slipped Half-Hitch (9.2.2) would be used to lock off a Munter Hitch. (For a Slipped Half-Hitch it may be advisable to add an extra hitch with the loop of the slip.) The safest is simply to secure the eye of the slip with a second carabiner.
b) attaching blocks and lowering devices; two Half-Hitches are an appropriate back up for the knot (5.10.3).

Pluses:
a) always available
b) When locked off, this knot is a multi-talent. It is secure regardless of the direction of pull; quick to tie and untie

Minuses:
a) Adding friction with the Munter Hitch puts extra strain on the rope due to major twisting. It is advisable, especially in figure 5.10.2, to use a large pear shaped carabiner.
b) Otherwise I'm still searching.

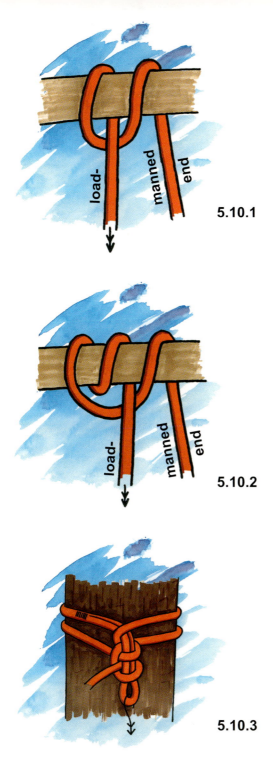

6. Bends

Worth Noting:
There is no need to make things harder than they really are.

A bend connects at least two ropes either at the ends or at the rope middle.

6.1 Overhand Bend

Explanation: very simple

Use: If one or two ropes need to be pulled up into the tree and one rope end is available, then and only then is this a good knot. Should only be used if the rope will not be loaded.

Pluses: fast

Minuses: eventually hard to untie after being pulled tight; it is possible to attach it mid-line simply by tying with a bight, but the result is a very bulky knot.

6.2 Water Knot & Flemish Bend

Other names: The Flemish Bend is also a Figure-Eight Bend or a Ring Bend.

Explanation: The Water Knot starts with an Overhand Knot (2.1). The second end is then, starting at the opposite end, run parallel to the first rope (6.2.1).
The Flemish Bend is tied the same only started with a Figure-Eight Knot (2.3) as in figures 6.2.2 and 6.2.3.

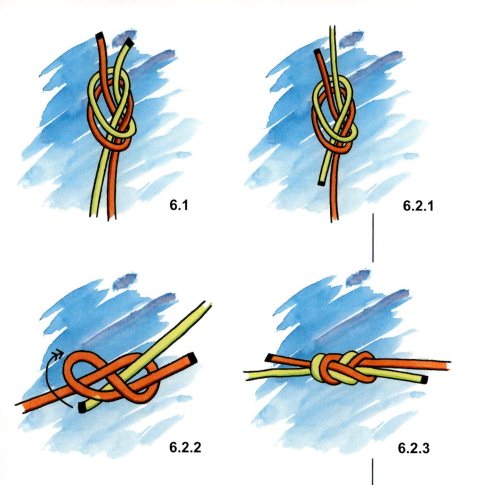

Use: a bend for long term use, i.e.: an endless webbing sling

Pluses: Both ends point in the direction of pull. Both are small knots, the Water Knot being the smaller.

Minuses: The process of running the ends parallel is time consuming; hard to open after being pulled tight although this is less so with the Flemish Bend

Worth Noting:
Because several accidents have occurred with this knot, it is advisable either to use the Beer Knot (6.7) or preferably a professionally sewn webbing sling.

6.3 Sheet Bend and Double-Sheet Bend

Other names: Figures 6.3.1 and 6.3.2 are both examples of weavers knots.

Explanation: works with two ends or with one end coming in mid-line on another rope (6.3.1); either tied like a Bowline (4.5), or pulled together with the trick in figure 6.3.2; warning: every trick has its dangers, so make sure that the loose end is stuck through the eye of a Simple Noose (3.1). Which direction it enters is unimportant (the difference being a Left-hand or a Right-hand Sheet Bend (ref. 8.1)), but if it is a Slipknot's (2.4) eye that you are using, the result is quite different (6.3.3). This is the Lock Knot.
Double-Sheet Bend (6.3.4): Instead of the above "one", make two single turns, one after the other. Tuck the end as with the Bowline (4.5). Notice that with different rope thickness, the smaller rope makes the round turn (1.5).

Use: the suitable knot for fastening ropes that need to be pulled up

Pluses: quick to tie, even mid-rope; easy to untie

Minuses: lowers drastically the braking strain of a rope; do not use as an end to end tie off for climbing or heavy loads.

Worth Noting:
The Double-Sheet Bend is more secure than a simple Sheet Bend. If a rope needs to be pulled up and there is a fear that the Sheet Bend will open, then one can secure the loose end with a Half-Hitch (9.2).

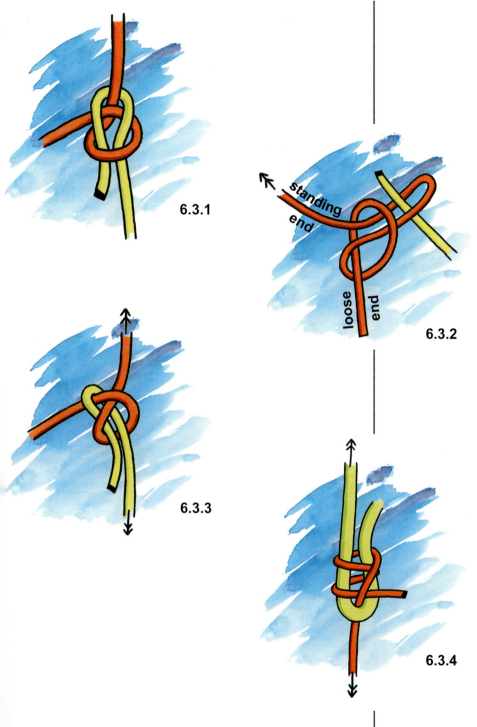

6.4 Quick Hitch

Explanation: as shown; it is the Lock Knot (6.3.3), with a slip.

Use: solely for pulling up ropes

Pluses: the best knot for this job; can bind mid-rope to mid-rope

6.4

6.5 Double-Fisherman's Knot

Other name: Grapevine Knot

Explanation: Run two ends from opposite sides parallel to each other. With the ends tie Barrel Knots (9.4) around their respective standing ends as in figure 6.5.1.

Use: the standard knot for prusik loops

Pluses: high security

Minuses: hard to untie

Worth Noting:
Make sure that both ends are secured and not that two Barrel Knots are in one end. It looks the same but is a recipe for disaster. Another nice variation for a footlock sling is the Sliding Double-Fisherman's Knot (6.5.2); tied as above as a loop, simply with the loop side opposite the knot captured in the Barrel Knots. The advantage is the two adjustable eyes. It is necessary that both eyes are under load, otherwise the knot can open (6.5.2)

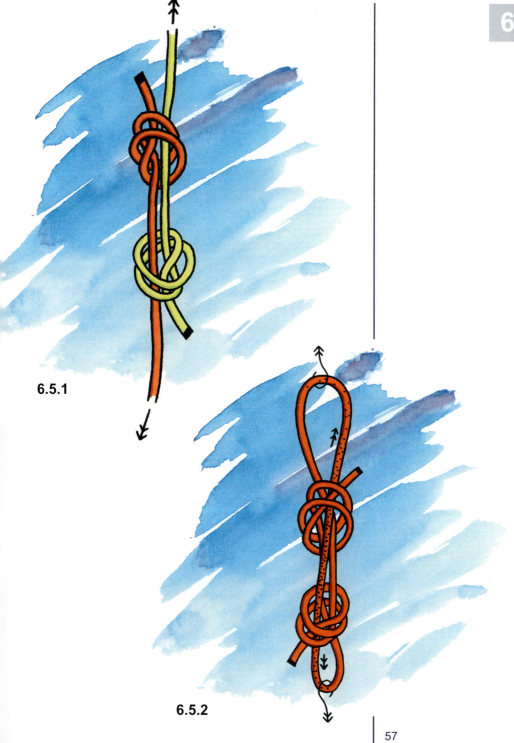

6.5.1

6.5.2

6.6 Double-Buntline

Worth Noting:
I was thinking that I had come up with this knot all on my own until Benedikt Goldbeck, told me that he had seen it on a Danish diagram of knots. If anyone has more info, please contact me.
The results of the load tests are available to the public at www.kletterdienste.de (special thanks to Edelmann and Ridder for their friendly support).

Other names: newly named if not a first appearance

Explanation: This is a mix of the Buntline (5.8) and Double-Fisherman's Knot (6.5): Each end is fixed to its respective rope with a self locking Clove Hitch (5.1.3); can also be tied mid-rope (6.6.1)

Use: This is a good bend when the ropes are going to experience some heavy loading but still need to be untied. Because the Double-Buntline can be tied mid-rope, it can be used to form a large loop for a static removable false crotch (6.6.2). In reference to the Sliding Double-Fisherman's Knot (6.5.2), one could just as well tie a Sliding Double-Buntline (6.6.3). This snugs up even better on a carabiner. The warning to figure 6.5.2 also applies here.

Pluses: easy to open

Minuses: at first an awkward knot to tie

6.6.2

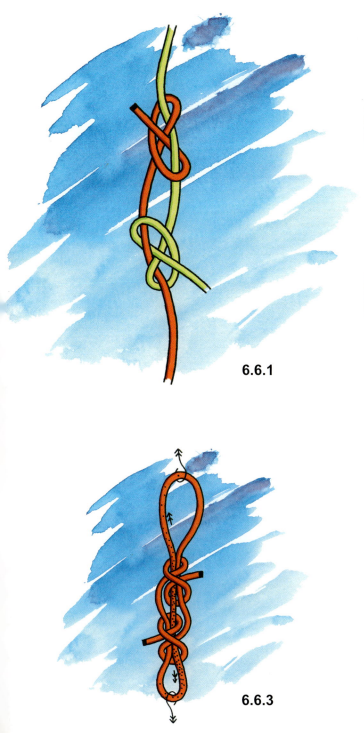

6.6.1

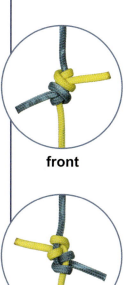

front

back

6.6.3

6.7 Beer Knot

Explanation: Tie a loose Overhand Knot (2.1) in the webbing. Stick one end of the webbing into the other (at least 12 times the width of the webbing). Push the knot around the sling until it is in the middle of the doubled webbing and pull the knot tight.

Use: a long lasting bend for webbing

Pluses: The ends don't get in the way; minimal reduction in the breaking strain

Minuses: The ends are out of sight; only useful for webbing

Worth Noting:
If the Overhand Knot is seen as the ropes whipping, then this is almost a splice.

6.7

Climber's Friction Hitches 7

7 Climber's Friction Hitches

A friction hitch attaches rope to an object (usually a thicker rope), which remains inactive in tying the knot. The climber's friction hitch acts as a rope grab or a self-belaying ascending and descending device.

Friction hitches are the cream of the crop under the tree knots. They have many variations. What I have picked out are the most used knots in the profession, plus a few extra. Many of the knots are very similar, so that a change in one gives a variation of another.

The loose ends of the friction hitches are either bent together so as to form a loop, or they are separately tied to a carabiner with a Double-Fisherman's Loop (3.3), like the Very Happy (7.10).

Most of the diagrams could be either seen as a frontal view or a back view. Furthermore, the mirror image of each is fully legitimate, but for climbing knots that have little distance between the climber and his rope, the choice may hamper the effectiveness (especially when a Double-Fisherman's Loop is tied into a small lift pulley (for example: "Fixe" from Petzl or "Easy" from Edelrid)).

Most of the knots here can be used in a "long" or "short" form, with the exceptions of the Hansa Hitch (7.5.2) which only works long, and the

Machard (7.6), the Very Happy (7.10) and the Valdotain Braid (7.12), which all must be kept short.

A comment on the Drawings: It may be found, especially with the quick knots (those that easily ascend and descend even with bodyweight hanging in them), but also with others, that they do not function as well as imagined even when carried out as diagramed. The type and condition of the material can have an extreme effect on its working properties. Simply an incorrect length of the accessory cord can hinder the proper working of a knot. The number of turns can have monumental effects. Thus I would always suggest (especially with the quick knots) that new knots be gradually and carefully brought into use, because they all have very specific qualities. Start low and slow.

It is also mandatory that the knot is tested for its functionality (i.e. is it easy to loosen, does it clamp shut when full bodyweight falls in it. These qualities are often in conflict with each other.

By using quicker knots, safety is marginalized. This must be recompensed with careful climbing.

Excluding the Blake (7.4), all diagrams depict the use of 8-9 mm accessory cord on a 12-13 mm climbing rope.

7

7.1 Prusik

Explanation: Starting with a Girth Hitch (5.6), the turns of the rope are simply continued. 3 turns of the loop is the norm.

Use: the beginner's climber's hitch; used as a tension minding lock in a mechanical advantage system; can also be used on horizontal lines

Pluses: very safe; easy; symmetrical (functions equally in both directions)

Minuses: sometimes too much of a good thing

Worth Noting:
One should be able to tie this knot with the eyes covered, behind the back and under water. Climbing can be a very enjoyable experience with the Prusik, as long as it is orderly attended (optimally well spaced turns).

7.1

7.2 Swabian Prusik

Other name: Asymmetrical Prusik

Explanation: There should be five parts of the cord encircling the climbing rope. It is important that more turns are in the upper half than in the lower half. After practice, four turns as opposed to five may render an improved climbing experience (naturally taking the material into account).

Use: beginner climber's hitch level two

Pluses: improved upward advancement compared to the Prusik (7.1)

Minuses: can't be tied with a sling

Worth Noting:
Once you've got the taste of a better friction hitch, it's hard to stop here.

7.2

7.3 Klemheist

Explanation: If three turns are sufficient for the Prusik, then four turns are required here.

Use: used as a self-belay when ascending with footlock, or descending with an eight

Pluses: quicker to tie and easier to open then a Prusik

Minuses: The Klemheist grips by bending the rope. This bend however is relatively hard, which makes it unsuitable for climbing. Under heavy load (a mechanical advantage system), it can flip over on itself becoming practically impossible to open.

Worth Noting: a small but interesting range of uses

7.4 Blake

Explanation: If four turns are not sufficient, more are allowed (my record is ten), but note that the loose end is always tucked under the first two turns (7.4.1). It is usual to tie this knot with material of the same diameter as the climbing line.

Use: As a climber's hitch in a traditional climbing system it can be tied with the loose end of an end of line attachment (for example: Clove Hitch (5.1)) (7.4.2). One may attach it to a rope already under load (perhaps with a few more turns); for spider legs (7.4.3): As a secondary support, you can use a 9 mm cord (approx. 5 m long). It should be noted that the rigging rope be tied closer to the

Worth Noting: Jason Blake made this knot famous and possibly invented it. However, it is used proficiently and for a longer time by the Lumberjacks around the Italian village of Belluno. In Italian it is known as the "Belluno Knot".

7.3

7.4.3

7.4.1

7.4.2

center of gravity than the secondary rope, and that angle α should be as small as possible, not exceeding 120 degrees. If there remains the danger of a rotation of the branch, it is always possible to tie in another spider leg. Refer also to Blake Loop (4.11).

Pluses: vast number of uses

Minuses: Who knows?

7.5 Bachmann Hitch and Hansa Hitch

Other name: Carabiner Hitch

Use: either can be used as a climber's hitch, but the Hansa Hitch (7.5.2) is the better choice; if you want to get fancy: to attach a removable redirect pulley. Tie a ripcord to the carabiner in the Bachmann Hitch (7.5.1). For this use it is preferable to the Blake (7.4).

Figure 7.5.2 shows the Hansa Hitch for beginners: A: Bachmann Hitch, B: Lift (hang a 6 mm thick prusik sling under the first turn of the Bachmann), C: Stopper knot for the lift.

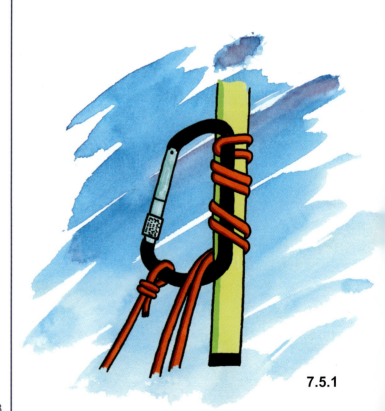

7.5.1

With a built-in ripcord the Hansa Hitch reaches its peak, a level equal to a long form of the Lock Jack, but should only be used by experienced climbers. For further information check www.kletterdienste.de.

Pluses: easy to loosen even after heavy loading; possibilities for a ripcord and an effective prusik lift

Minuses: It is a little jolty, making smooth starts and brakes are difficult.

Worth Noting:
a knot for the precisionist with a wild side; those who use it will reap the benefits.

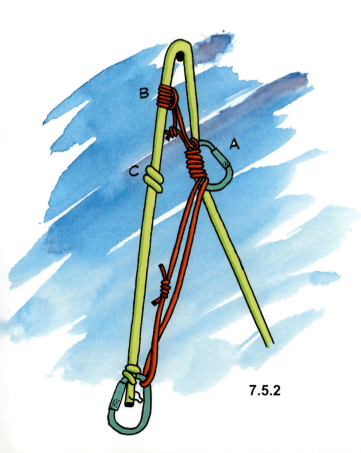

7.5.2

7.6 Machard

Other names: possibly many

Explanation: Make five to six turns with a loop and hook both ends into a carabiner. Pay attention that the end to end tie off in the loop is well situated as shown.

Use: There are a number of uses for this knot:
1. to attach a mechanical advancement system to a rigging rope,
2. as a rope minding knot in a mechanical advancement system,
3. on a horizontal rope and
4. for a removable in line system on a footlock rope. This is very useful in a rescue situation as well as for short term climbing use. The footlock sling is replaced with the Machard and your climbing system adjusted to be the same length as your normal footlock sling. The Machard acts as a friction saver. At point "A" in the diagram hangs a small ring. At point "B" hangs a large ring. After footlocking to the required height on the footlock rope, one can simply stop and start to work with the climbing system. It is important that the Machard locks under load (check it on the ground and add an extra turn if necessary). Just as important is that the climbing rope doesn't rub on the ascension rope. This is uncommon but still check it. Getting the system out of the tree runs as usual.

Pluses: distribution of weight into four strands; easiest friction hitch to tie; always easy to loosen

Worth Noting:
This one is a must know. If the Machard is tied with a longer sling, the upper part of the doubled-cord can slip down forming crosses (ref. Valdotain Braid (7.12)). One of the crossing doubled-up cords always bridges the other. If the care is taken that the bridging cords alternate, one has a Machard Braid (not illustrated). With a single cord, as opposed to the doubled-up cord of a sling, by adding eyes at either end (for example the Double-Fisherman's Loop (3.3)) and applying the same tying methods as above, one receives comparatively either the Valdotain (not illustrated) or the Valdotain Braid.

Minuses: If it is loosely tied and should slowly receive bodyweight, be sure that it closes tightly, unaided. The Machard needs more turns than other hitches for it not to slip.

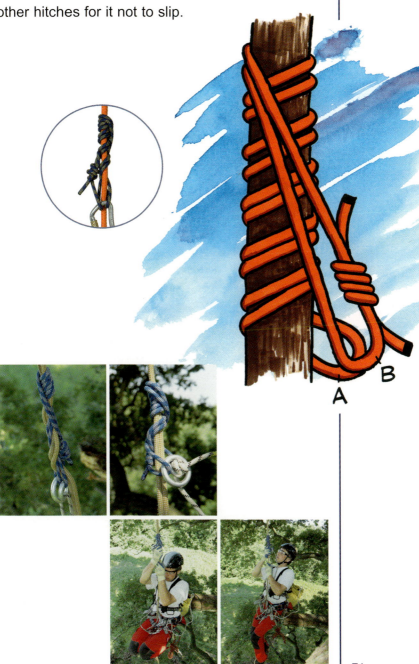

7.6

7.7 Distel

Explanation: This is a Clove Hitch (5.1) with three extra turns in the upper strand. When you become accustomed to the knot, you may find yourself tying it differently.

Use: This is beginner climber's hitch level three (1. Prusik (7.1) and 2. Swabian Prusik (7.2)). Shortened form, in combination with a pulley, works well for a flipline.

Pluses: quick but still in safe limits; due to its close relationship to the Clove Hitch, it is easy to learn.

Minuses: too quick for some

Worth Noting: gets its name from Uli Distel

7.7

7.8 Saxon Prusik

Explanation: a small but crucial difference to the Swabian Prusik (7.2)

Use: climber's hitch

Pluses: It's quicker.

Minuses: all the negative aspects that quickness brings with it

Worth Noting:
Matthias Goede and Bernhard Schütte from the tree-care company Happy Tree, developed this hitch claiming to tie the Knut (7.13).

7.8

7.9 Happy

Other names: If you even want to know, the inventor originally called it the Die Happy, no thanks.

Explanation: If the Saxon Prusik (7.8) is the evolution of the Swabian Prusik (7.2), then this is the evolution of the Distel (7.7).

Use: up and down

Pluses: quicker

Minuses: Refer to the Saxon Prusik (7.8).

Worth Noting:
This hitch was propagated by Matthias Goede and Bernhard Schütte from the tree-care company Happy Tree.

7.9

7.10 Very Happy

Other names: also known as Die Very Happy; still a first appearance

Explanation: similar to the Happy (7.9), with the lower strand left long enough to loop and be tucked under itself with a stopper knot

Use: climber's hitch

Pluses: It always bothered me that the Happy sometimes crunched together and became sticky. This variation can be stretched and thus the speed can be better regulated.

Minuses: It is more cumbersome to tie.

Worth Noting:
The so-called "stopper variation" also improves the Distel (7.7), the Saxon (7.8), and the Knut (7.13), i.e.: Very Distel, Very Saxon and Very Knut???

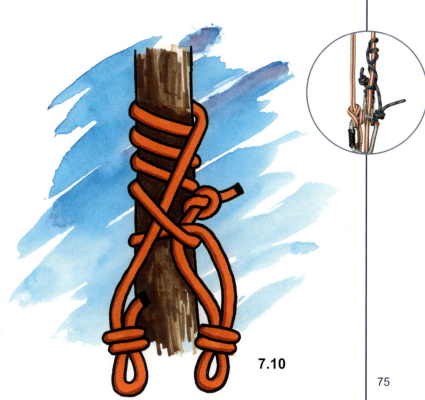

7.10

7.11 Howard Hitch

Explanation: the Distel (7.7) with a few (maybe three) turns around the bridging strand

Use: climber's hitch

Pluses: The extra turns act as a spring, helping the hitch to remain loose.

Minuses: Refer to the Very Happy (7.10).

Worth Noting:
Thanks goes to Paul Howard for this one.

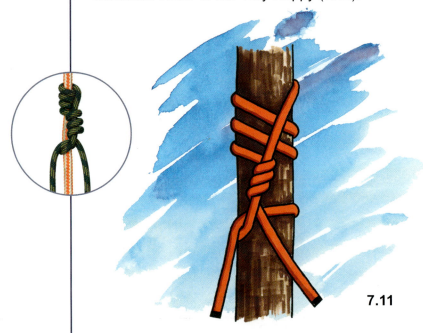

7.11

7.12 Valdotain Braid

Other names: French Prusik; This is incorrectly known to some as the Machard (7.6), under which the difference is described.

Explanation: There is more than one way to tie this hitch. Pictured below are three turns and four crosses, two on each side of the rope. The number of turns, the number of crosses, as well as the length of the cord are all variables that are very sensitive to change.

Use: climber's hitch; competition worthy hitch; works well even on a stiff support rope

Pluses: very fast!

Minuses: too fast for beginners; can cause the rope to twist; this hitch can stretch out, making it possibly hard to reach. Compared to other hitches, this one is the most likely to have problems tightening on its own, requiring an occasional incentive. (In German it is called the "Streichelknoten" (Caressing Hitch).)

Worth Noting:
Handle with care! As long as you know what you're doing, this is an excellent climber's hitch.

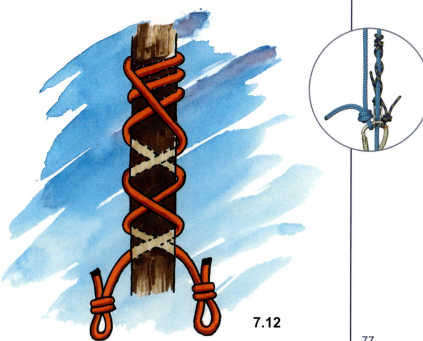

7.12

7.13 Knut

Explanation: almost the Happy (7.9), with a change in the lowest turn

Use: not solely for descending

Pluses: quick

Minuses: quick

Worth Noting:
Thanks goes to Knut Foppe for this one.

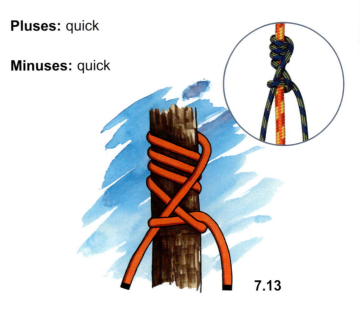

7.13

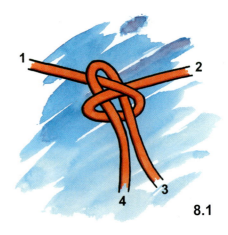

8.1

Various

8.1 Met one, met 'em all

You've seen the Sheet Bend, Lock Knot, Quick Hitch, Bowline, and Eskimo Bowline. Here they are again, all in one diagram.

1. **Right-hand Sheet Bend:** pull on 1 and 4
2. **Left-hand Sheet Bend:** pull on 1 and 3
3. **Right-hand Sheet Bend with a slip:** (not yet described) pull on 1 and 4, 2 is slipped
4. **Left-hand Sheet Bend with a slip:** (not yet described) pull on 1 and 3, 2 is slipped
5. **Right-hand Lock Knot:** pull on 2 and 3
6. **Left-hand Lock Knot:** pull on 2 and 4
7. **Right-hand Quick Hitch:** pull on 2 and 3, 1 is slipped
8. **Left-hand Quick Hitch:** pull on 2 and 4, 1 is slipped
9. **Right-hand Bowline:** pull on 1 and the loop from 2 and 4
10. **Left-hand Bowline:** pull on 1 and the loop from 2 and 3
11. **Right-hand Eskimo Bowline:** pull on 2 and the a loop from 1 and 3
12. **Left-hand Eskimo Bowline:** pull on 2 and the loop from 1 and 4

(Etc. etc. etc)

Right handed is always the more secure variation. Whether there is a difference in the braking strain is still undecided.

8.2 Bread and Butter

Other Names: a new name, maybe a first appearance but not a new invention

Explanation: Like the name says, "spread" the rope back and forth over your hand, fold it over and pack it tight: three times around to the left and three to the right (8.2.1 and 8.2.2). The length of the rope used is dependent on the distance that needs to be thrown (see "Use"). Practice makes perfect.

Use: to throw a rope end over something; take the Bread and Butter, with enough rope coils for it to reach the target. Ideally the bundle should unwind on the other side of the targeted branch. If the bundle is tight enough, by lightly pulling the rope as the bundle unwinds, you can bring the rope to swing, and with practice it is possible to have the unwound rope end land back in your hand like well-thrown Boomerang.

Pluses: easy cheesy; compared to other knots this one completely unwinds. If you have a bad throw, it is easy to pull the loose rope through even the tightest forks.

Minuses: not the finest of rope work

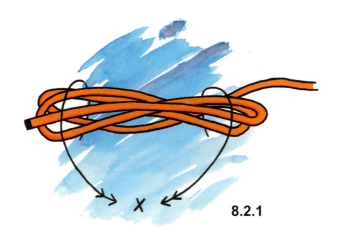

8.2.1

8.2.2

8.3 Gasket Hitch

Explanation: either laid in the hand or over the shoulders; the rope is thrown alternately in loops left and right. A few turns around the whole holds it all snug. A loop made with the loose end is slipped through the eye of the bundle and then around the head and pulled tight (8.3.1-8.3.3).

Pluses: The rope won't tangle. The bundle holds its form. The rope unwinds without problems when the bundle is opened; a good way to dry ropes

Worth Noting: Despite all of its benefits, it is advisable over a certain rope length to use a rope bag.

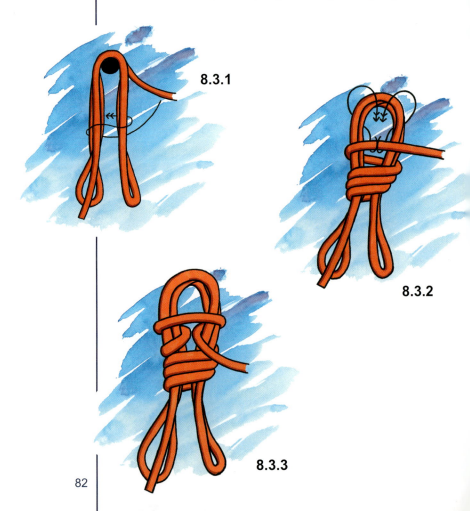

8.3.1

8.3.2

8.3.3

Safety Knots   9

What always seems to be coming into question is: "Do knots really need to be additionally secured?" The answer is situation dependent: How secure does the knot have to be to fulfill the intended use? How long will the knot be active? Is it holding a person or material? How heavy is the load? What sort of rope is being knotted? (A stiff rope often needs to be secured, because it can't be pulled as snug as a softer more pliable rope.)
I've picked out five safety knots that could secure all the knots in this book (the Yosemite-Tie Off (4.6) is naturally a special case). Back up knots are almost always a job for the loose end, well, almost. The Half-Hitch (9.2) on the Timber Hitch (5.3) is in the standing end, but still a back up knot.

In the following drawings, it is always a Double-Fisherman's Loop (3.3) that needs to be secured. This was a random decision placing the emphasis on the safety knot. In reality, the Double-Fisherman's Loop rarely needs securing.

9.1 Stopper Knots

Tying a stopper knot in the loose end is usually sufficient security. For a short action the pictured Overhand Knot (2.1) is more often than not an excellent solution. For example by smaller branches rigged with the Clove Hitch (5.1) or the Timber Hitch (5.3). For the Blake (7.4) I would recommend the Figure-Eight Knot (2.3) or a Double-Overhand Knot (2.2) assuming that one is climbing for a longer period of time.

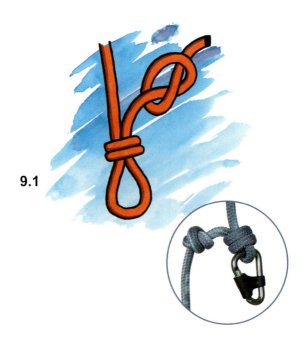

9.1

9.2 Half-Hitch and Slipped Half-Hitch

The Half-Hitch (9.2.1) is quick to tie but just as quick to untie itself. None the less it is often enough, for example with the Cow Hitch (5.7). Two Half-Hitches are a heightened security. Three Half-Hitches, however, borderlines fooling around, and might imply that a different safety knot is required.

Figure 9.2.2 is a Slipped Half-Hitch. A second slipped Half-Hitch gives additional security. Because it can be tied mid-line it is a good back up for the Munter Hitch (5.10).

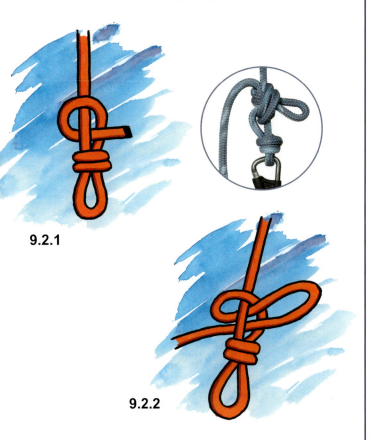

9.2.1

9.2.2

9.3 Half-Knot and Single-Bow

The Half-Knot is an Overhand Knot (2.1) tied around an object, i.e. the standing end of the rope (9.3.1). Compared to the Half-Hitch (9.2), security is drastically improved. If the knot remains inactive (as with the anchor point for high access technicians or as a back up for an access line anchored around a tree trunk), the Half-Knot will do the job (for example the Bowline (4.5.3)).

The Single-Bow (9.3.2), which is a slipped Half-Knot, can be used as a back up for the Munter Hitch (5.10). It is best to secure the eye to the standing end of the rope with a carabiner. This is a back up that can be tied mid-line. To keep the record straight: The Slipped Noose (3.2) is a turn secured with a Single-Bow.

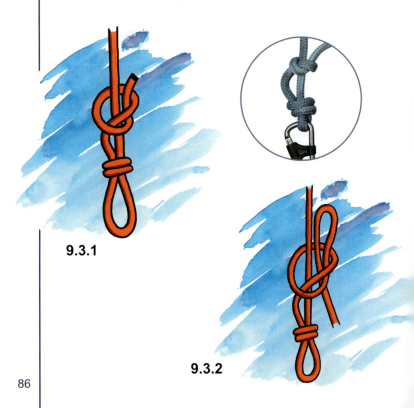

9.3.1

9.3.2

9.4 Barrel Knot

This Double-Overhand Knot (2.2) tied around the standing end of the rope is the ultimate safety knot. For any knot that is in a dynamic system, this is the security choice.

If a knot finally isn't secure, maybe it doesn't lie on the safety knot but rather on the original choice of knot.

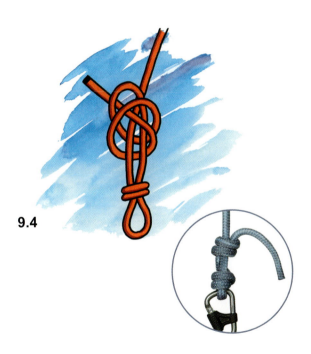

9.4

10 Sources

The best sources are competent colleagues. In the recent past I have crossed paths with many. Here I would like to extend my gratitude for all the help and critique.

There are numerous books on the subject knots. Because this isn't a scientific work, I will note only the most important:

Ashley, Clifford W. The Ashley book of knots. Doubleday. 1944

11 Thanks

I would like to thank all those who supported this book. First of all I thank my wife Pauline, whose patience was tried with my many knots and who always stood by me, ready with constructive criticism.

I would furthermore like to thank Johannes Bilharz and Friedrich Drayer for the editing. Without their help a lot of questions might have gone unanswered.

Cutting Edge Solutions

www.climb-ART.com